# RELIGION VIOLENCE & PEACE

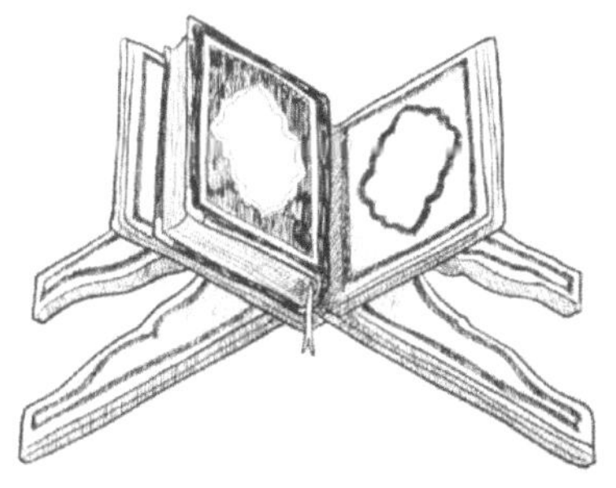

Written By:
Emmanuel Usanga

# ACKKNOWLEDGEMENT

We would like to express our sincere gratitude to all those who have supported us in the creation of this book, "Religion, Violence, and Peace."

Firstly, we would like to thank our families and loved ones for their unwavering support and encouragement throughout this project. Their love and understanding have been a constant source of inspiration and motivation.

We are deeply grateful to the scholars, researchers, and experts who have contributed their valuable insights and perspectives to this book. Their expertise and dedication have enriched our understanding of the complex issues at the heart of this work.

We would also like to thank our colleagues and friends for their support and guidance throughout the writing process. Their feedback and encouragement have been instrumental in shaping this book.

We are grateful to the publishers and editorial team who have worked tirelessly to bring this book to fruition. Their professionalism and commitment to excellence have been invaluable.

Finally, we would like to express our gratitude to all those who have been affected by religious violence and conflict. It is our hope that this book contributes to a deeper understanding of the complex issues at play and inspires new avenues for dialogue and collaboration towards peace and reconciliation.

Cover design by: Central Park Designs

Typesetting by: Central Park Edits

# INTRODUCTION

Religion is often seen as a source of conflict and violence, but it can also be a source of peace and reconciliation. The relationship between religion and violence is complex and multifaceted, and many factors contribute to the use of religion as a justification for violent acts.

Religion for many years has been a powerful force in shaping the beliefs and actions of individuals and societies throughout history. From peaceful practices to violent conflicts, religion has played a pivotal role in promoting both peace and violence.

Religion comes from two Latin words "re" which means again and "lig" which means to connect. Thus, the common translation of the term is to "join again" or "reconnect". There is no single definition of religion as scholars all over the world have tried to define this concept. Michael Molly (2013) defines religion as the joining of our human world to the sacred world. Molly saw that religion is a way of life of a set of people, thus, suggesting that a "spiritual path" would be more fitting to religion.

One important factor is the interpretation of religious texts and teachings. Some interpretations of religious texts can be used to justify violence, while others emphasize peace and compassion. It is important to recognize that there are many different interpretations of religious texts and that these interpretations can change over time.

Misinterpretation of some concepts in a certain religion is one of the greatest factors that brings about conflict in a different religion. People who practice their religion feel that religion is only a belief system and fail to put into consideration that religion is mainly an inward step; worship of one supreme being inward.

Another factor is the political and social context in which religion is practiced. In some cases, religion has been used as a tool by those in power to justify violence and oppression. In other cases, religious leaders and communities have played a key role in promoting peace and justice.

Religion, violence, and peace are three concepts that have been intertwined throughout human history. While religion has been a source of inspiration for many peaceful movements and has provided a moral compass for individuals and communities seeking to live in harmony with one another, it has also been used to justify acts of violence and conflict, leading to wars and other forms of social unrest.

The relationship between religion, violence, and peace raises important questions about the role of religion in promoting or hindering peace. It also highlights the need for a deeper understanding of how religious beliefs and practices can shape individuals and societies, and the impact that this can have on peacebuilding efforts.

Finally, the relationship between religion, violence, and peace is shaped by the actions of individuals and communities. It is up to us to choose how we interpret and practice our faith, and to work towards a more peaceful and just world. By promoting dialogue, understanding, and respect between different religious traditions, we can build bridges of peace and create a more harmonious world for all.

# THE RELATIONSHIP BETWEEN RELIGION AND VIOLENCE

The relationship between religion and violence is complex and multifaceted. While some religions espouse peaceful principles, others have been associated with acts of violence throughout history. It is important to note that religion itself is not the cause of violence, but rather the way in which it is interpreted and practiced by individuals and groups.

There are many different ways to think about the relationship between religion and violence. On one hand, some people may see religion as the root of all violence, as it is often used to justify wars and other acts of aggression. On the other hand, others may see religion as a force for peace, as it can provide people with a moral compass and a sense of community.

It is important to remember that religious beliefs are not always the sole cause of violence. Many factors contribute to violent behaviour, such as political instability, economic inequality, and social injustice. However, religion can be a powerful tool that is used to legitimize or condone violence.

In some cases, religious leaders may openly encourage their followers to engage in acts of violence. This can be seen in extremist groups who use religious rhetoric to justify their actions. In other cases, people may use their religious beliefs to rationalize violent behaviour that they would otherwise not consider. This has been seen in numerous conflicts throughout history, including the Crusades, the Spanish Inquisition, and more recent examples like the conflict between Israel and Palestine.

On the other hand, many religious communities have been at the forefront of peacebuilding efforts and promoting nonviolence. Religious leaders and organizations have played a significant role in conflict resolution and reconciliation in many parts of the world.

It is therefore important to critically examine the role that religion plays in promoting peace or violence and to recognize that both positive and negative relationships exist. It is also important to distinguish between the actions of individuals and groups who claim to represent religion and the larger teachings and principles of that religion itself.

Ultimately, the relationship between religion and violence is complex and nuanced. There is no simple answer as to whether religion is a force for good or evil. It depends on how religious beliefs are interpreted and applied by individuals and groups.

# **CRITICISMS OF RELIGION**

Criticism of religion has been a part of human society for a long time. There are many reasons why individuals and groups criticize religion. Here are some of them:

1. Lack of scientific evidence - Some people criticize religions for being based on unproven beliefs and for lacking scientific evidence to support certain beliefs.

The lack of scientific evidence is sometimes used as a criticism of religious beliefs, particularly when religious claims conflict with scientific findings. For example, some religious beliefs might conflict with established scientific theories, such as the theory of evolution or the Big Bang theory. In such cases, critics argue that religious beliefs lack empirical evidence and are therefore less credible than scientific theories.

However, it is important to know that not all religious beliefs are intended to be scientific claims. Some beliefs are based on personal experiences or cultural traditions, and do not necessarily require scientific evidence to be considered valid. Moreover, some religious believers argue that the lack of scientific evidence does not necessarily mean that their beliefs are untrue or invalid, since scientific methods may not be appropriate for testing certain types of claims.

2. Social progress – Social progress is one of the criticisms of religion, particularly when religious beliefs and practices are seen as hindering or impeding progress in areas such as human rights, gender equality, and scientific advancement. For example, some religious beliefs and practices have been used to justify discrimination against certain groups, such as women, LGBTQ+ individuals, and people of different faiths. In such cases, critics argue that religion is a barrier to social progress and that religious leaders and institutions must adapt to changing social norms and values.

However, it is important to note that religion has also been a driving force for social progress in many cases. For example, religious leaders and organizations have played important roles in promoting humanitarian causes, such as poverty reduction, disaster relief, and peacebuilding. Moreover, some religious beliefs and practices have been used to inspire social movements for justice and equality, such as the civil rights movement in the United States.

Ultimately, whether or not religion is a hindrance or a catalyst for social progress depends on the specific beliefs and practices in question, and the context in which they are being evaluated. It is important to approach any debate or discussion with an open mind and a willingness to consider different perspectives.

3. Inconsistencies - Inconsistency is sometimes used as a criticism of religion, particularly when religious beliefs and practices appear to be contradictory or inconsistent with each other. For example, some religious texts may contain conflicting or contradictory messages, or religious leaders may interpret religious teachings in different ways, leading to disagreements and divisions within religious communities.

Critics may argue that the inconsistency of religion undermines its credibility and makes it difficult to take religious claims seriously. They may also point out that inconsistencies in religious teachings and practices can lead to confusion, conflict, and even violence within and between religious groups.

It is important to note that religious beliefs and practices are shaped by a variety of factors, including historical context, cultural traditions, and individual interpretations. Moreover, many religious believers see inconsistencies as a natural part of the human experience, and may view them as opportunities for personal growth and spiritual development.

In the end, the particular religious practices and beliefs under consideration, as well as the context in which they are being analysed, will determine whether or not inconsistency is a legitimate criticism of religion. Any discussion or debate should be entered into with an open mind and a readiness to examine opposing viewpoints.

4. Fundamentalism - Fundamentalism is a term that can be used to describe a particular type of religious belief and practice. Fundamentalism refers to the strict adherence to religious values and beliefs. This can lead to intolerance towards people who hold different views or believe in different religions.

While fundamentalism can be a criticism of religion in some contexts, it is not necessarily a criticism of religion as a whole. Some people may view fundamentalism as a positive expression of religious devotion and a way to preserve traditional beliefs and practices. Others may criticize fundamentalism as being too rigid and limiting, and may argue that it can lead to intolerance, extremism, and conflict.

5. Violence - Violence can certainly be a criticism of religion, particularly when religious beliefs and practices are used to justify or incite acts of violence. There have been numerous instances throughout history where individuals or groups have committed acts of violence in the name of religion,

often against those who hold different beliefs or are perceived as threatening to the religious community.

Some critics of religion argue that the very nature of religious belief, with its emphasis on absolute truth and divine authority, can make it more prone to violence and intolerance. They point to religious conflicts throughout history, such as the Crusades or the Inquisition, as examples of how religion can be used to justify violence and persecution.

However, it is important to note that not all religious believers or communities engage in violent behaviour, and many religious traditions explicitly reject violence as a means of achieving their goals. Furthermore, violence is not unique to religion, and can be found in many contexts where people hold strong ideological or political beliefs.

In conclusion, while violence can be a criticism of religion, it is not necessarily an inherent feature of religious belief and practice, and should not be used to stereotype or condemn all religious believers or communities.

# **<u>RELIGION AND ITS ELEMENTS</u>**

According to Molly in classical Latin, *"religio"* means "awe for the gods and concern for poor rituals". However, it must be noted that it was the Western world that popularized the term religion. For this reason, it is not proper to apply the term religion according to cultures. Thus, Molly suggests the term "Spiritual path" as a more fitting designation to refer to other religious systems.

Religion can be defined as a system of beliefs and practices that are centred on the worship of a supernatural deity. Here are some elements that are often present in various religions:

Foremost of these key elements is the "belief systems". When we say belief systems we are specifically speaking about the "worldview" of a particular group of people, hence a belief system refers to a complete interpretation of the universe (Physical and spiritual) and the human beings and the role they play. That is a reason in any kind of religion there is always a dynamic relationship between the world and humans. For example, how the Taoism highly values "Nature"

Another important element of religion is the "community". A religion always involves a group of people who shows the same belief system and practice the ideals. A certain religion cannot be called a religion in the strict sense of the word if it doesn't have a community of believers. Some religions such as Islam and Protestantism, are so aggressive in expanding their membership.

Number three on the list of elements of religion is "ritual". Religion has always enacted beliefs that were made real through ceremonies. A great example is the Roman Catholic church, which always starts any prayer with the sign of the cross, the Muslims on the other hand place their foreheads on the ground as a sign of submission to God.

Fourth is "ethics". As we may already know, ethics is a major branch of philosophy that deals with the morality of human behaviour. In religion, ethics has to be established. In other words, there should be rules of human behaviour that govern the activity and actions of the community of believers. For instance, for the adherents of the Christian domination, the Jehovah Witness, blood transfusion is always wrong. Or in Christianity in general, polygamy is generally viewed wrong while in Islam, it is viewed as morally right. This explains why we have what we call "Buddhist ethics", "Islam ethics" and "Christian ethics".

The fifth characteristic or element of religion is an emotional experience. As it is well-known religion is always characterized by emotional experiences such as dreads, guilt, awes, devotion, and liberation.

Sacred texts and teaching is another element of religion. Many religions have a set of sacred texts or teachings that guide their followers on how to live their lives and achieve spiritual fulfilment. Examples of such texts include the Bible, Quran, and Bhagavad Gita.

Religion has all of the benefits in life, but, according to social conflict theory, it can also reinforce and promote social inequality and social conflict. Karl Marx who is regarded as the father of social conflict theory said that religion was the "opiate of the masses" (Marx, 1964). By this, he meant that religion, like a drug, makes people happy with their existing conditions.

# NATURE OF DECISION-MAKING REGARDING PEACE AND VIOLENCE

Religious decision-making regarding peace and violence can vary widely depending on the specific religious belief system and its interpretation by different individuals and groups.

Some religions, such as Buddhism, emphasize nonviolence and peaceful conflict resolution. In Buddhism, the principle of non-harming, or ahimsa, is central to the religion, and violence is seen as a violation of this principle. Similarly, Jainism also emphasizes nonviolence and the avoidance of harm to all living beings.

Other religions, such as Christianity and Islam, have more complex views on peace and violence. While both religions contain teachings on peace and love, they also contain passages that can be interpreted as justifying violence in certain circumstances, such as self-defence or the defence of one's community. Interpretations of these passages can vary widely among different individuals and groups within these religions.

In general, religious decision-making regarding peace and violence is influenced by a number of factors, including the specific religious teachings, the cultural and historical context in which the religion is practiced, the political and social circumstances of the time, and the individual beliefs and values of the adherents of the religion.

# <u>RELIGIOUS VIOLENCE</u>

Violence according to the Oxford dictionary is a behaviour involving physical force intended to hurt, damage, or kill someone or something. Violence is a multifaceted and complex issue that can take on many forms, such as physical, verbal, emotional, and psychological. It can be a result of many factors including social, political, cultural, and economic ones. Violence often can have devastating consequences, including physical harm, emotional trauma, and loss of life.

Religious violence is a complex phenomenon that can encompass a wide range of violent actions that are motivated by religious beliefs. The roots of religious violence may be traced to various factors such as territorial and resource competition, ethnic strife, and power struggles among religious communities.

Hormby (2006) defines religious conflict as a situation in which religious adherents are involved in a serious disagreement or argument between one religious group and another. This is a situation in which there is opposition in ideas, opinions, feelings, and wishes.

Sadhguru in his YouTube video said that: "When one believes in something the person will want to impose it on other people and when people resist it the imposer will want to force it on them". Forcing it may be by war or conflict it can also be by money, policies, false preaching, and lots more. Religious violence occurs when there is hatred for one's religion. This can occur internally which leads to splitting and the existence of different churches in one religion. Jealousy and favouritism are also other factors that bring about religious conflict.

Religious violence may include acts such as sectarian violence, terrorism, persecution of minority religions, and holy wars. Holy wars, also known as religious wars, usually involve violent conflicts fought with the goal of advancing or defending one's religious beliefs. These types of wars are usually fought over sacred or religious sites or to control the theological narrative of a region.

Most violence happens in its religion example Christianity because of the misconception of a certainly believe system. The existence of many Pentecostal churches is a result of not agreeing to a particular belief or pattern of worship. For example, the Lutheran Church was founded in the early sixteenth century when a German monk, Martin Luther, was against the Roman Catholic Church's practice of selling indulgences as part of the penance, or punishment, for those who sinned against church teachings.

Religious violence can be fuelled by various influences including political, economic, and social factors. It can also be justified by religious dogma or by interpreting religious texts through the lens of violence. However, it is important to distinguish between violence that is motivated by religious beliefs and violence perpetrated by individuals or groups using religion as a justification for their actions.

One perspective of religious violence often arises when individuals or groups feel threatened or marginalized, and they use their religious beliefs as a means to justify or legitimize their actions. This can be seen in instances where religious extremism fuels conflicts between different groups, such as the ongoing conflicts in the Middle East between Sunni and Shia Muslims. A good example is the case of Boko Haram in Nigeria. Boko Haram means "Western Education is forbidden". Boko Haram is an Islamic sect founded by Mohammed Yusuf in 2002 that wants to purge Nigeria by making it an Islamic state ruled by Sharia law. Boko Haram is against Western education because it is slowly replacing their way of education and that was what led to the kidnap of the Chobok girls on 14th April 2014.

Another upshot of violence in religion is the lack of peace. In this context, it doesn't just mean peace in society but also peace of mind. In a society where there is a dominating religion in terms of population and such religion is always causing violence, fighting people who do not join their religion, always favouring people from their religion, and lots more.

Overall, religious violence is a complex phenomenon that is difficult to understand and address. To truly tackle this issue, a multi-faceted approach is required that involves education, social awareness, and strong leadership that fosters respect, tolerance, and understanding.

## Types of Religious Violence.

Religious violence can take many forms and can be perpetrated by individuals, groups, or even states. Here are a few examples of types of religious violence:
1. Inter-religious violence
2. Intra-religious violence
3. Sectarian violence

**Inter-Religious Violence:**

Inter-religious conflict can be defined as conducted or involving or existing between two or more religious groups or movements. In other words, most religious conflicts usually develop into inter-ethnic conflicts even where and when they started as purely religious disagreements. For example, Muslims VS Christians

## Intra-Religious Violence:

Intra-religious conflict can be defined as conducted or involving or existing within a particular religious group or movement. These are religious conflicts that within a particular religion that are rooted in differences resulting from religious matters.

## Sectarian Violence:

In understanding what sectarian conflict is, it is paramount to have an understanding of what sectarianism is. Sectarianism can be defined as a form of bigotry, discrimination, or hatred arising from attaching relations of inferiority and superiority to differences between subdivisions within a group. Common examples are denominations of a religion, ethnic identity, class, or region for citizens of a state and factions of a political movement.

Sectarian violence and/or sectarian strife is a form of communal violence inspired by sectarianism, that is, between different sects of one particular mode of ideology or religion within a nation/community. Religious segregation often plays a role in sectarian violence. Examples of sectarian violence include; the Shiites and Sunin Sects like the Boko Haram Insurgent group in Nigeria.

-

# PEACE

Peace is a fundamental concept in many religions and is often viewed as a central goal or ideal. Many religious traditions promote peace as a way to achieve harmony and unity among people, and to create a more just and compassionate world.

In Christianity, peace is seen as a gift from God and is often associated with the teachings of Jesus Christ. The Bible teaches that peace comes from faith in God and that believers should work to promote peace in the world by loving their neighbours and enemies, forgiving others, and practicing nonviolence.

In Islam, peace is a central concept, and the Arabic word for peace, "salaam," is used as a greeting. Muslims believe that peace comes from submission to the will of God and that believers should strive to establish peace and justice in the world through acts of compassion, charity, and social justice.

In Buddhism, peace is seen as the ultimate goal of spiritual practice and is often associated with the concept of Nirvana, or enlightenment. Buddhists believe that peace comes from letting go of attachment and desire and that by cultivating compassion and wisdom, individuals can find inner peace and contribute to a more peaceful world.

In Hinduism, peace is seen as a natural state of being, and is often associated with the concept of "Shanti," or inner peace. Hindus believe that peace comes from living in harmony with the natural world and that by practicing yoga, meditation, and other spiritual practices, individuals can cultivate inner peace and promote peace in the world.

There are many other religious traditions that promote peace as a central value, including Sikhism, Judaism, and Taoism. While the specific teachings and practices of each religion may differ, the idea of peace as a fundamental human value is a common thread that runs through many spiritual traditions.

Religion can play an important role in promoting peace in our societies. Peace is a concept of social friendship and harmony in the absence of hostility and violence. In other words, peace is a term against violence and war. Religious teachings, beliefs, and practices can provide a moral and ethical framework for understanding and addressing conflicts.

There are many ways in which religion can promote peace, including:

Fellowship of Reunion: This is an interfaith organization that recognizes the essential unity of all creation, works toward a just and peaceful world, and recognizes the transformative potential of religion in realizing such a vision. Additionally, religious peace-making is becoming more common and the number of cases cited is growing at an increasing pace.

Unity: Religious leaders should use all means necessary the fostering unity among all people. Unity is the state of being united or working together towards a common goal. It is a powerful force that can bring people together and create positive change in the world. When people are united, they can accomplish great things. They can solve complex problems, overcome obstacles, and achieve common goals. Unity brings together people of different backgrounds, cultures, and beliefs, and helps them find common ground and shared values.

Interfaith dialogue: This is one form of religious peace-making. Rather than seeking to resolve a particular conflict, it aims to defuse interfaith tensions that may cause future conflict or derive from a previous conflict. Interfaith dialogue is expanding even in places where interreligious tensions are highest. Not infrequently, the most contentious interfaith relationships can provide the context for the most meaningful and productive exchanges.

Trust: Another way of bringing peace amongst people of different religions is by building relationships of trust with people of other religions. According to the Oxford dictionary, trust is a firm belief in the reliability, truth, or ability of someone or something. Trust is a powerful concept that underlies all successful relationships, whether personal or professional. It is the foundation upon which we build connections with others, and it is essential to our well-being and sense of security. However, trust is not something that can be given lightly, and it must be earned through consistent actions and behaviours. Trust is what promotes unity and peace in society. When a religion trusts another religion with the capacity of controlling power in the right manner, then will there be peace.

Encouraging forgiveness: Forgiveness is a key theme in many religions and is often seen as a way to heal relationships and promote reconciliation. By forgiving others and seeking forgiveness for one's own mistakes, individuals can move past conflict and work towards peace.

Supporting Social Justice: Many religions call for the pursuit of social justice and the protection of human rights. By working to address issues such as poverty, inequality, and discrimination, individuals can help create more equitable and peaceful societies.

Praying for peace: In many religious traditions, prayer is seen as a powerful tool for promoting peace. By praying for peace and sending positive intentions out into the world, individuals can contribute to a more peaceful and harmonious global community.

These are just a few examples of how religion can promote peace. Ultimately, the specific ways in which religion can contribute to peace will depend on the beliefs, values, and practices of each individual and community.

# CONFLICT RESLUTION

Conflict resolution in religion refers to the process of resolving disagreements, disputes, or conflicts that arise among individuals or groups within a religious context. It involves using techniques and strategies to help individuals or groups work together to find a mutually acceptable solution to their differences.

Many religions have their own specific approaches to conflict resolution, but there are some common principles that are shared across different faiths. These include:

1. Active listening: This involves listening carefully to the concerns and perspectives of others without interrupting or judging them. It is important to ensure that everyone has the opportunity to express their views and to feel heard.

Active listening is an important component of conflict resolution in religion. It involves listening carefully to the concerns and perspectives of others without interrupting or judging them. This allows individuals to feel heard and understood, and can help to create an environment of mutual respect and empathy.

In a religious context, active listening can be particularly important because disagreements often arise over deeply held beliefs and values. When individuals feel that their beliefs are being dismissed or misunderstood, it can exacerbate the conflict and make it more difficult to find a resolution.

By actively listening to others, individuals can build trust, promote understanding, and create a more positive environment for resolving conflicts. This can be particularly important in a religious context, where disagreements can be deeply personal and emotionally charged.

2. Respect: Showing respect for others and their beliefs is crucial in resolving conflicts in a religious context. This includes respecting the dignity and worth of every individual, even if their views or beliefs differ from our own.

Respect is a fundamental principle in conflict resolution in religion. It involves showing consideration and regard for the dignity and worth of every individual, even if their views or beliefs differ from our own. In a religious context, respect is particularly important because many conflicts arise over deeply held beliefs and values.

By showing respect for others, individuals can create an environment of mutual trust and understanding, which is essential for resolving conflicts in a religious context. Respect can help to create a sense of empathy and connection, and can promote a willingness to work together to find a mutually acceptable solution. This can be particularly important in situations where there are deeply held differences, as respect can help to create a foundation for dialogue and reconciliation.

3. Collaboration: Collaboration can be a powerful tool in conflict resolution in religion. When people from different religious backgrounds work together, it can promote understanding, respect, and empathy. This can help to break down barriers and reduce tensions between communities.

One effective way to promote collaboration in conflict resolution is through interfaith dialogue. Interfaith dialogue involves people from different religions coming together to discuss their beliefs, values, and experiences. This can help to build bridges between communities and create opportunities for joint action on issues of common concern.

Another approach to collaboration in conflict resolution is through mediation. Mediation involves a neutral third-party facilitating discussions between conflicting parties to help them reach a mutually acceptable resolution. Mediators can help to create a safe and respectful environment for dialogue and can also help to identify common ground between conflicting parties.

In addition to interfaith dialogue and mediation, there are many other ways to promote collaboration in conflict resolution in religion. These may include community-building activities, joint social justice initiatives, and educational programs that promote understanding and respect for different religious and cultural traditions. Ultimately, the key to successful collaboration in conflict resolution is a commitment to mutual respect, empathy, and a willingness to work together towards a common goal.

4. Forgiveness: Forgiveness can play an important role in conflict resolution in religion. Many religious traditions emphasize the importance of forgiveness as a means of promoting healing and reconciliation in the aftermath of conflict.

In many cases, forgiveness can be a difficult and painful process, especially when there has been significant harm or injustice. However, many religious traditions teach that forgiveness is essential for personal healing and spiritual growth, as well as for promoting peace and reconciliation in the broader community.

Forgiveness can take many forms, depending on the religious tradition and the nature of the conflict. In some cases, forgiveness may involve letting go of anger and resentment towards those who have caused harm. In other cases, forgiveness may involve seeking reconciliation with those who have been harmed, and working to repair the damage that has been done.

In many religious traditions, forgiveness is seen as an act of compassion and mercy, rather than a form of weakness or surrender. By extending forgiveness to others, individuals can demonstrate their commitment to the values of their faith, and promote healing and reconciliation in their communities.

Of course, forgiveness is not always possible or appropriate in every situation. In cases where harm or injustice has been severe or ongoing, forgiveness may be a long and difficult process, and it may not be possible to fully restore relationships or repair the damage that has been done. However, even in these cases, a commitment to forgiveness and reconciliation can help to promote healing and prevent further harm or conflict.

5. Mediation: Mediation can be a valuable tool in conflict resolution in religion. Mediation involves a neutral third party facilitating discussions between conflicting parties to help them reach a mutually acceptable resolution. Mediation can be particularly effective in religious conflicts, where emotions can run high and communication can break down.

Mediators can help to create a safe and respectful environment for dialogue and can also help to identify common ground between conflicting parties. They can encourage parties to listen to each other's perspectives, express their own needs and interests, and work together to find creative solutions to complex problems.

In religious conflicts, mediators may also be able to draw on their knowledge of religious traditions and values to help parties find common ground. They may be able to identify areas of shared belief or practice, or help parties understand how their religious beliefs may be influencing their perceptions of the conflict.

Mediation can also be a less confrontational and adversarial approach than traditional legal or political methods of conflict resolution. By working together in a collaborative process, parties may be more likely to find resolutions that are acceptable to all sides, and that promote healing and reconciliation.

Of course, mediation is not always appropriate or effective in every situation. In some cases, parties may be unwilling or unable to engage in dialogue, or the power dynamics between parties may be too unequal for mediation to be successful. However, in many cases, mediation can be a valuable tool for resolving religious conflicts and promoting peace and understanding between communities.

Overall, conflict resolution in a religious context involves a commitment to dialogue, understanding, and reconciliation. It requires a willingness to listen to others, to respect their differences, and to work together to find common ground and promote peaceful coexistence.

# CONCLUSION

The relationship between religion, violence, and peace is complex and multifaceted. While some argue that religion is a source of violence and conflict, others believe that it can be a force for peace and reconciliation.

It is important to acknowledge that religion has been used to justify violence throughout history and that religious extremists continue to perpetrate acts of violence in the name of their faith. However, it is also important to recognize that many religious traditions prioritize peace, justice, and compassion, and that religious leaders and communities have played an important role in promoting nonviolence and conflict resolution.

To promote peace and reduce violence, it is essential to engage in interfaith dialogue and promote understanding and respect across religious lines. This can involve listening to and learning from different religious perspectives, as well as working together to address issues of common concern, such as poverty, inequality, and environmental degradation.

In the long run, achieving peace requires a multifaceted approach that addresses the root causes of conflict, including social, economic, and political factors. While religion can play an important role in promoting peace, it is essential to recognize that it is just one piece of the puzzle.

# <u>REFERENCES</u>


Emerson, M. O., Monahan, S. C., & Mirola, W. A. (2011). Religion matters: What sociology teaches us about religion in our world. Upper Saddle River, NJ: Prentice Hall.

Klassen, P. (Ed.). (2009). Women and religion. New York, NY: Routledge.

Marx, K. (1964). Karl Marx: Selected writings in sociology and social philosophy (T. B. Bottomore, Trans.). New York, NY: McGraw-Hill.

Moberg, D. O. (2008). Spirituality and aging: Research and implications. Journal of Religion, Spirituality & Aging, 20, 95–134.

Morris, A. (1984). The origins of the civil rights movement: Black communities organizing for change. New York, NY: Free Press.

Terry, K., & Smith, M. L. (2006). The nature and scope of sexual abuse of minors by Catholic priests and deacons in the United States: Supplementary data analysis. Washington, DC: United States Conference of Catholic Bishops.

https://www.georgiaencyclopedia.org/articles/arts-culture/lutheran-church

Gundy-Volf, J. (1998, September–October). Neither biblical nor just: Southern Baptists and the subordination of women. Sojourners, 12–13.

https://www.usip.org/publications/2008/02/religion-world-affairs-its-role-conflict-and-peace

Darren Grem (2017, July 26) Lutheran Church

Philo Notes (May 24, 2022) What is Religion? Definition and Characteristics. https://philonotes.com/2022/05/what-is-religion-definition-and-characteristics

United State Institute for Peace (February 1st, 2008) Religion in World Affairs: Its Role in Conflict and Peace

Sadhguru (2013) Why Religion and Conflict? https://www.youtube.com/watch?v=ZxoxPap PxXk

www.ingramcontent.com/pod-product-compliance
Lightning Source LLC
Chambersburg PA
CBHW061608250726
48657CB00017B/2268